Original title:
Asteroid Epics

Copyright © 2025 Creative Arts Management OÜ
All rights reserved.

Author: Oliver Bennett
ISBN HARDBACK: 978-1-80567-769-7
ISBN PAPERBACK: 978-1-80567-890-8

In Search of Cosmic Wonders

Zooming through the galaxy,
With my trusty flying spoon,
Looking for a cosmic snack,
Maybe cheese that's shaped like moon.

Planets twirling, stars that wink,
Caught a comet, it said 'hi!'
Said it's on a diet now,
But I still want to give it a fry.

Floating near a giant rock,
Held my breath, what a sight!
Turns out it was just a shoe,
That twinkled in the light.

Chasing trails of glowing dust,
With a giggle and a cheer,
I'm convinced there's pizza pie,
In the stratosphere so near.

Dodging meteors with flair,
Wearing shades, feeling bold,
Trying to catch a space raccoon,
Now that's a tale to be told!

Between the Stars We Dream

In the cosmos, squirrels float,
Searching for acorns in a boat.
They wear tiny helmets, quite absurd,
Singing space songs, oh what a world!

Aliens dance with glittery shoes,
Juggling planets, sharing their blues.
They giggle and laugh, what a delight,
Under the glow of a moonbeam light.

Night Skies and Cosmic Reveries

Comets race like dreamy cats,
Chasing their tails in celestial hats.
Stars wink slyly, plotting a prank,
While moons trip lightly to the cosmic bank.

Galaxies swirl in candy cane hues,
As meteors whistle the latest news.
Cosmic cupcakes float all around,
With sprinkles of laughter that astound.

The Timeless Celestial Parade

Planets march in a silly line,
Wobbling and bobbling, looking divine.
Uranus has a tutu, bright and pink,
While Saturn's rings are a reason to wink.

The Sun leads with a goofy grin,
Shooting out rays, where do we begin?
Pluto peeks out, what a shy friend,
In this parade, laughs never end!

Waking the Celestial Spirits

Stars snooze soundly on soft, fluffy beds,
Dreaming of cookies and noodles for heads.
A cosmic alarm clock starts to ring,
Waking them up for a morning fling.

Nebulas giggle, tugging on clouds,
While comets shout jokes, drawing a crowd.
As the galaxies stretch, oh what a sight,
With cosmic capers, day turns to night.

Legends of the Galactic Voyage

In the void where space cats play,
Stars throw parties night and day.
Dancing comets in a line,
Wobble, giggle, and then dine.

Green men with five legs prance,
Twirl around in cosmic dance.
Singing songs of fizzy drinks,
While the meteor shower winks.

Robots chase their own loose screws,
While aliens wear funny shoes.
They all laugh 'til they can't breathe,
In this universe of make-believe.

Giant squids in rocket ships,
Spilling snacks with funny quips.
Their laughter echoes through the stars,
As they cruise by Saturn's bars.

Odyssey through the Cosmic Veil

Wormholes lead to dance-off nights,
With space whales challenging flights.
Bouncing meteors say, "Hey dude!"
As planetary wolves share food.

Galaxies spin like a top,
While the aliens holler, "Don't stop!"
Floating past in bubble cars,
Making wishes on bright stars.

A cosmic ball is quite absurd,
With robot jokes that sound like birds.
Extraterrestrial chefs compete,
Cooking dishes that taste like feet.

And when the night is full of cheer,
Time to calculate some beer.
The universe is bright and bold,
With laughter worth its weight in gold.

Celestial Fireflies

In the night sky fireflies twirl,
Creating chaos with a swirl.
Zany antics on the go,
Lighting up the stardust flow.

A butterfly with rocket wings,
Singing songs of cosmic flings.
Ticklish stars poke fun at moons,
While space frogs sing silly tunes.

A comet slips on cosmic goo,
While others join in swirling too.
Beware the giggling black holes,
For they swallow all the good rolls.

Friends in space laugh with delight,
Sharing stories through the night.
Celestial fun in every beam,
Our universe, one big dream!

The Journey of Lost Celestials

Lost in space, a group of clowns,
Zooming past the goofy towns.
Galactic wigs on giant heads,
Crashing into soft bed spreads.

Rocket cars with squeaky wheels,
Fill the vacuum with joyful squeals.
Stellar jokes that tickle hearts,
Even light years can't keep them apart.

Silly aliens sell their wares,
Interplanetary stuffed bears.
Playing tag with bouncing stars,
Escaping from the space bazars.

With laughter bright and galaxies wide,
Their friendship is the universe's pride.
So join the fun, don't miss the show,
For every cosmic smile will glow!

Celestial Wanderers

In the sky they roam around,
Bouncing off with goofy sound.
Space rocks tripping through the night,
Crumbling jokes in their flight.

With a wink, they clash and dive,
Juggling stars, they come alive.
Galactic giggles, meteor trails,
Zooming past on cosmic sails.

They scoop the dust from Saturn's rings,
Rehearsing goofy cosmic things.
Slipping past with silly grace,
These wandering stones embrace the space.

When they crash, it's quite the scene,
Like a rock band, loud and mean.
In the dark, their laughter rolls,
A concert for the cosmic souls.

Dance of the Cosmic Rocks

Watch them twirl and spin about,
Chunky stones with a joyful shout.
They leap and bound through starry haze,
In celestial clubs, they're always on blaze.

With a shuffle and a flip, oh my,
Meteor two-step, flying high.
Each rotation, a stellar flair,
Gravitational tango in the air.

Solar flares join the jive,
Making sure the groove's alive.
"Step to the left!" one does declare,
While burying space in a cosmic chair.

In a waltz around Mars, they play,
Not a care in their rocky ballet.
With laughter bright, they dance and sway,
Cosmic rocks having their fun all day.

Tales from the Celestial Veil

Gather 'round and hear the tale,
Of rocks who danced on a comet's trail.
With goofy grins, and a stellar vibe,
These cosmic jokers twirl and jibe.

They spin through void, a frosty breeze,
Trading puns with such great ease.
In the dark, their stories unfold,
Gravity's mischief, a joy to behold.

From craters big to moons so bright,
Their wild antics fill the night.
"Did you hear the one about the sun?"
They laugh, as their cosmic race is run.

Chasing comets like they're pets,
Playing tag, no serious threats.
With each crash, a punchline gleams,
In the cosmos, they're the kings of dreams.

The Silent Voyage of Stone

Drifting silently through the sky,
With a smirk, these rocks fly by.
No sound but laughter in their wake,
As they joke about the paths they take.

In their voyage, a wink or two,
Comets wave like, "See ya, dude!"
With each roll, a story's spun,
About how they all had a cosmic run.

Floating gently, a game of hide,
On a moon's back, they love to glide.
"Catch me if you can!" one shouts with glee,
While the galaxy chuckles merrily.

With a twist and turn, they make a mess,
Almost like they couldn't care less.
These stones of fun, in orbits roam,
All while plotting their cosmic home.

The Celestial Remnants

In space, there's a rock with a funny face,
It rolls through the cosmos at its own pace.
With craters like giggles and dust for a smile,
It bounces and tumbles, amusing all the while.

Its buddies are comets, they zoom by so fast,
They wave from afar as they hurl past.
But our silly rock just laughs all day,
Saying, 'Catch me if you can,' in its own cheeky way.

Chasing Shadows in Infinite Space

There's a light in the dark that plays hide and seek,
Chasing shadows of dreams that are just a bit weak.
A planet dressed in pajamas, so cozy and warm,
Snoozes through space, far from any alarm.

A star sneezes brightly, creating a flare,
The rock rolls its eyes, 'Whatever, I swear!'
With laughter that echoes through the void so wide,
It joins in the chase, bouncing with pride.

Celestial Musings on the Edge of Night

On the edge of the cosmos, where the wild things play,
A little rock juggles moonbeams all day.
It slips on stardust, it giggles with glee,
Creating new dances, oh what a sight to see!

A satellite whispers, 'You're having too much fun!'
But the rock just chuckles, 'Wait till we run!'
The universe chuckles, it's a humorous game,
Where laughter and starlight call rocks by their name.

Collision Course

Two rocks met one day with a fumble and roll,
They bumped and they jostled, both lost control.
With a twinkle and twist, they tumbled through space,
Shouting, 'We're stars! Look at our grace!'

They sparkled like fireflies, despite the big crash,
Now they orbit each other, making a splash.
In the galaxy's play, they dance without care,
Creating a story that lightyears will share.

The Poetry of Orbit and Time

In a dance up in the sky,
Planets spin and satellites fly.
One wobbles left, another tumbles right,
Chasing tails in cosmic light.

Comets sport a flashy tail,
While rocks just float with little detail.
Each one's got a story, oh so bright,
Yet none can find their way at night.

Lament for the Lost Wanderers

Oh, the wanderers lost in space,
Floating 'round with zero grace.
They took a wrong turn, what a ride!
Now they're stuck on this cosmic slide.

With every spin, they wish to land,
But gravity's stricter than they planned.
And where's their map? They've lost it too,
Now just playing tag with a cosmic goo.

Starlit Epics of Ancient Solitude

In the silent depths of night,
Stars complain, "What a fright!
Forever glowing, never still,
Sharing secrets, against their will."

The ancient dust feels so alone,
Whispers in a monotone.
"Oh, to be a planet round,
With friends and dances to be found!"

The Song of Cosmic Travelers

Travelers sing a silly tune,
Bouncing off the man in the moon.
With a dip and dive, they twirl in space,
Juggling stars in a wild race.

"Catch me if you can!" they cry,
As meteors zoom and comets fly.
Through rings of Saturn, they weave and spin,
In this cosmic carnival, let the fun begin!

The Destiny of Rogue Bodies

In space, they dance with no regard,
A swarm of rocks, their moves are hard.
They slide and glide in cosmic play,
But often crash, what a messy day!

One dodges Earth with style so sleek,
But trips on Venus, oh what a freak!
They spin like tops, those cosmic fools,
Not knowing gravity's the king of rules.

With craters deep, their stories told,
Each bump and bruise a challenge bold.
They giggle through the galaxy wide,
As asteroids roll on a wild ride.

So raise a toast to these merry sights,
Who swirl and twirl on endless nights.
In every tale of cosmic cheer,
The rogue bodies waltz, no need to fear!

Legends of the Galactic Trail

In the realm where stars ignite,
Strange rocks chase comets in their flight.
They hum a tune, a bumpy beat,
While dodging planets, oh so sweet.

A legend tells of one oh-so-sly,
Who aimed for Mars but missed, oh my!
Instead, it found a nice, warm sun,
And claimed it as its victory run.

These chunky heroes, wild and rare,
With tales of chaos, flair, and air.
They tell of journeys through the void,
Where every bang is so enjoyed.

So laugh with us at this quirky band,
Who roam the cosmos, completely canned.
For every bump is just a chance,
For planets and rocks to join the dance!

Silence Between the Stars

In the dark where silence reigns,
A meteor zooms, breaking chains.
It sneezes loud, and off it goes,
While stardust giggles in rows.

Each void holds secrets, whispers slight,
As chunks of rock race out of sight.
One trips and tumbles, what a scene!
"Did you see that?" the starlight beams!

With every zip and zany laugh,
They plot their course, a cosmic path.
"Whoops! Too close!" comes the cosmic call,
Then off they zoom, twice as tall.

The quiet night, it softly hums,
As space rocks play their silly drums.
The universe holds a chuckle or two,
As silence echoes, and laughter pursues!

Oracles of the Dark Beyond

In depths of space, with twinkling light,
Rocks tell tales of endless night.
They're sages wise, with secrets aged,
But trip on facts, now disengaged.

"Watch out!" one yells, and spins around,
A prophecy lost in a cosmic bound.
Yet through the chaos, wisdom flows,
In clunky language, the cosmos knows.

With every crash, a laugh is sparked,
These oracles, remarkably stark.
They bumble through their timeless rants,
Creating fables of starry chants.

So heed the rocks with a playful grin,
For in their mischief, wisdom can begin.
In the dark beyond, they shine and play,
Their oracles live in a comical way!

Fragments from the Cosmos

In the sky, a rock does dance,
With a wobble and a prance.
It trips on stars, oh what a sight,
As space farts burst with pure delight.

A chunk of dust with dreams so big,
Looks for planets, does a jig.
"Hey there, Earth! Wanna be my friend?"
But all it meets is cosmic wind.

It rolls through voids, a comic scene,
Like marbles lost, so rarely seen.
Such silly paths, it can't deny,
As moons just laugh and wink on by.

In the end, it might collide,
With a comet taking pride.
A meeting odd, such fate to greet,
A cosmic giggle, can't be beat!

The Path of Forgotten Wanderers

Once a pebble, now a ball,
On a journey, it had a call.
"To the sun!" it said with glee,
But veered off course, what a spree!

Ducked by Saturn, missed by Mars,
It thought it could wish on stars.
"I'm just a rock with big dreams,"
It rolled on, plotting funny schemes.

It met a comet, hair like foam,
Together they decided to roam.
"Let's play chase and cause a fuss!"
While dodging the galaxy's bus.

Now in space, they skip and play,
Inventing games to pass the day.
Forgotten rocks, with laughter bright,
The universe loves a silly flight!

A Symphony of Silence

In the void, not a sound to be found,
Yet with stardust, there's magic around.
A comet whispers, a planet sighs,
While quasar giggles fill the skies.

Black holes wobble, just take a peek,
Making goofy faces, oh so cheek.
The silence hums a gentle tune,
While black dwarf stars sport hats and balloons.

Neutron stars play a fast-paced game,
Chasing light, never quite the same.
A cosmic jam session, how hilarious,
The quiet universe turns quite joyous.

In this stillness where laughter grows,
The cosmos bursts with whimsical shows.
Stars twinkle, as if to declare,
Even silence knows how to share!

The Cosmic Ballet

Galaxies twirl in a grand ballet,
While stardust pirouettes all day.
Planets plummet with graceful flair,
As meteors leap, a true love affair.

The Milky Way's chorus sings a tune,
While moons do cha-cha 'neath the moon.
Dancers dip in a spiral whirl,
Cosmic partners, in starlight swirl.

Asteroids clumsy, trip on a star,
They tumble and giggle, near and far.
In this waltz, each twist is fun,
Ballet of planets, laughter won.

As comets cartwheel, the cosmos beams,
A stage of wonder, alive with dreams.
In cosmic rhythm, together they play,
In the universe's bright cabaret!

Voyage of the Void

In a spaceship of socks, we zoom and we glide,
Through cosmic confetti, on a bubble we ride.
With alien llamas and giggles galore,
We navigate starlight and open the door.

The map made of jelly, it leads us astray,
As comets throw parties and planets hold sway.
We tiptoe on planets, all wobbly and round,
While moon mice play tunes, it's a sight most profound.

A rocket made from a cereal box flew,
We holler and laugh, it's a riotous view.
With space hats that sparkle and rocket shoes bright,
We dance in the orbits, our joy takes flight.

On this voyage of nonsense, we frolic and play,
With hiccuping meteors, we sway and we sway.
A circus of chaos, the cosmos our friend,
With laughter the fuel—there's no need to pretend.

Stardust Journeys

We packed up our snacks for a trip to the sky,
With sandwiches floating, oh my, oh my!
The Milky Way diner serves coffee in cups,
While we catch shooting stars and start to hiccup.

In pajamas made of planets, we swerve and we spin,
Jumping over black holes with each silly grin.
Galactic balloons flying high with a cheer,
We laugh as we tumble, there's nothing to fear.

A cow jumped a comet, quite out of the blue,
With a wink from a star, it invited us too.
We rode on the tails of some glittery things,
As space kangaroos performed acrobatic flings.

In this universe wild, we're never alone,
With friends from the cosmos, we're making a home.
Through stardust and giggles, our journeys align,
Each laugh is a lightyear, together we shine.

The Great Cosmic Highway

On the Cosmic Highway, we zoom and we glide,
In a car made of marshmallows, full of wide-eyed pride.
With traffic of meteors and lights that glitter bright,
We honk with a laugh, it's a comical sight.

The GPS yells at us, 'Turn left past the sun,'
But we missed our exit, oh what a fun run!
With fuzzy aliens hitching a ride in the back,
We sing silly songs, not a single thing's lack.

Asteroids dancing like they're in a parade,
We join in the fun, our worries allayed.
Through tunnels of stardust and fog made of cheese,
We munch on the cosmos, it's a feast, if you please!

At the rest stop of laughter, we stretch and we roam,
With cosmic ice cream cones, feeling right at home.
The universe winks, with a twinkle so sly,
As we bounce down the road in our sweet, silly ride.

Echoes from the Beyond

Once in a while, we hear chuckles from space,
Where planets spin jokes at a merry fast pace.
The echoes of laughter swirl all around,
In the depths of the cosmos, the silly resounds.

An octopus juggles, in zero-g style,
As we float in our chairs, wearing smiles all the while.
With comets as confetti, we laugh and we cheer,
The galaxies whisper, 'Come join us, come near!'

A riddle from Saturn, it tickles our brains,
While orbiting dogs dance in cosmic terrains.
With each goofy giggle that bounces off stars,
We create our own laughter, no matter how far.

From the echoes we hear, a joy to be found,
In the cosmic embrace, where all love abounds.
So here's to the antics that shine in the night,
We're cosmic comedians, stars in our flight.

The Quest for Starlight

A traveler set out on a wild spree,
To catch a twinkle up in a tree.
With a net of dreams and a jar of glee,
He danced with shadows, oh so free!

The stars all giggled, and some flew away,
"You can't catch us! It's just play-play!"
Yet he tried and stumbled, a comical fray,
Creating a mess on that bright ballet.

He stumbled on stardust, fell into a bowl,
Sipped cosmic soup, lost all control.
With suns for dessert, oh, what a goal!
What a picnic it turned into! What a roll!

Still, he laughed and twirled in sparkly cheer,
For every flop brought him joy, oh dear!
He danced with the comets, no trace of fear,
Learning that fun is the grand souvenir!

Lullabies from the Skies

In the dark, the moon crooned low,
Singing to stars that sparkled aglow.
They giggled and wiggled, just putting on a show,
As meteors waved in their bright flow.

Clouds joined the chorus, a fluffy delight,
Mumbling sweet whispers of dreams taking flight.
Planets hummed softly, free of their plight,
Bouncing in rhythm, oh what a sight!

Starfish on comets threw wishes like darts,
Promising laughter would lighten our hearts.
Cosmic confetti flew, brightened our parts,
As night wrapped around us, and joy never departs!

So drift off to sleep as the galaxies sway,
While lullabies dance in the Milky Way.
For tomorrow brings more of the same playful play,
A universe giggling, come what may!

Guardians of the Night

The night watchmen, funny and bold,
Saunter on sidewalks with stories untold.
Wearing capes of stardust, in laughter they mold,
Protecting the dreams, both young and old.

With their trusty flashlights, they light up the gloom,
Chasing away shadows that threaten to bloom.
Fighting off fears with a plump rubber boom,
Creating a world full of magical room.

They tickle the edges of slumbering minds,
Riding on shooting stars, playful finds.
Grinning through galaxies, their joy unwinds,
Creating a night where silliness binds.

As dawn peeks in with a yawning stretch,
The guardians giggle, "Oh, what a sketch!"
With a twinkle, they vanish, but never forget,
That laughter in dreams is the best safety net!

Navigating the Unseen Cosmos

In a spaceship made of wishes and dreams,
A captain set sail on shimmering beams.
With a map drawn in crayon, oh, how it seems,
He giggled through nebulas and folly-filled themes.

Dodging space junk like it's just old news,
Mixing up orbits in sparkly blues.
Counting each planet, oh, what a ruse,
His compass kept spinning; what would he choose?

Every trip was a tale, a comical ride,
With aliens laughing at his wild side.
He'd wave and they'd chuckle, no need to hide,
In the unseen cosmos, adventure was wide!

So here's to the journeys, so wacky, so bold,
Finding joy in the strange, the new, and the old.
For laughter is stellar, and never gets cold,
In the universe's arms, let the stories unfold!

Castaway Comets in the Night.

Comets zooming through the sky,
Leaving trails as they fly by.
One lost its way, took a wrong turn,
Now it's charging up for a vacation burn.

It tried to land on a pizza pie,
But the crust just made it cry.
The cheese was hot, the pepperoni too,
Now it's orbiting the fridge, who knew?

Shooting stars are just in disguise,
Eloping with the moonlit fries.
They giggle as they dart and weave,
Forming constellations you wouldn't believe!

So next time you gaze at the night,
Watch for comets taking flight.
They're not just space rocks in a hurry,
They're out there having fun—don't worry!

Celestial Travelers

Planets shuffling on their way,
Trading tips for the perfect sway.
Jupiter said with endless pride,
"I've got more moons than a fancy guide!"

Mars tried to roast a cosmic s'more,
But Venus just rolled its eyes and swore.
"You call that a treat? You silly red dot!"
Then it fluffed clouds that were really hot.

Saturn, with its rings so grand,
Offers the best space disco band.
Pluto, feeling a tad too small,
Danced alone but still had a ball!

So if you see them on the move,
Remember the steps, let your body groove.
In this cosmic party, we all partake,
Even the stars like a good space cake!

Cosmic Whispers

Stars murmur secrets, sly and sweet,
Speaking of adventures on repeat.
One star boasted, shining so bright,
"I once played tag with a black hole at night!"

Galaxies giggled, swirling around,
Twirling like children lost and found.
They traded wishes like candy bars,
While comets rapped to the tune of guitars.

Satellites eavesdrop with a grin,
Listening closely, conjuring din.
A quasar whispered, "Take a break!"
"Let's throw a galactic cupcake bake!"

So don't you fret for the void of space,
Where laughter echoes, it's a happy place.
Join the fun, and you just might hear,
The cosmic tunes that tickle your ear!

Dance of the Celestial Stones

Pebbles in orbit, twirling about,
Joined a party they couldn't live without.
With cosmic beats that shook the crust,
They jived and spun, it was a must!

Meteorites strutted with style and flair,
Each one dazzling beyond compare.
They broke it down, from Earth to Mars,
Even the sun peeked out through stars!

Gravity bounced, trying to control,
But the dancers smiled, it took its toll.
They waltzed through the Milky Way's chocolate,
Sipping stardust from a comet's pocket.

So if you spot a rock taking flight,
Know it's dancing under the moonlight.
In the vastness where wonders awaken,
The stones are grooving, and never shaken!

The Celestial Tapestry

In the sky, a rock floats by,
Like a lost and confused pie.
It dodges planets, gives a wink,
'This ain't a game, what do you think?'

Through the cosmos, it rolls and spins,
Wearing a smile, where fun begins.
'Time for a dance!' it starts to shout,
While space dust gets them all kicked out!

With trails of glitter and sparkly fizz,
It jests 'I'm the best, everyone is!'.
A comet chases, can't keep the pace,
'Catch me if you can, my silly space!'

Bouncing off moons, it rocks the scene,
Dancing with aliens, feeling quite keen.
Yet lost in laughter, it turns and sways,
For nothing beats fun in cosmic ways.

Voyage Beyond the Stars

A spaceship sails through the bright night,
Captain Giggles full of delight.
With a crew of snacks and fizzy drinks,
They zoom through space, nobody thinks!

Bumping into Martians, who love to play,
'Trust us, we know how to race today!'
They zip around moons, with jelly beans,
Laughing so hard, bursting at the seams!

In a game of catch with space-time loops,
The crew of snacks form silly groups.
'Hey, who needs math when we've got fun?'
As they spin and twirl like a big cinnamon bun!

Back to Earth with stories to share,
Of cosmic blunders and jelly everywhere.
The crew lands laughing with raucous cheers,
This voyage was definitely worth the years!

Navigating Celestial Secrets

Navigating through stars, a map gone wrong,
The captain sings the silliest song.
With a compass made of candy and cheer,
They float past Black Holes, 'What's that, dear?'

Planets giggle, just out of reach,
Swirling in colors, a cosmic peach.
When they try to land, they bounce like springs,
The laughter echoes, oh, the joy it brings!

With meteor showers that tickle like rain,
They dance on comets, never feel pain.
They twirl with the stars, oh what a sight,
A celestial circus under moonlight!

When the journey ends, they spread cosmic cheer,
'Thanks for the giggles, till we meet here!'
With secrets to share, they sparkle and glow,
Fun in the universe, always on show!

Moments from the Cosmic Edge

In the vastness, where time takes flight,
A quirk named Zorp dances all night.
With twinkling toes and a cosmic grin,
It leaps through wonders, its journey begins!

Bouncing on stars, it plays peek-a-boo,
With the Moon as a partner, and Saturn too.
Each moment a giggle, each second a tease,
Zorp's got the universe rolling with ease!

When sunlight pops, the colors blend wild,
Like a toddler's dream, oh so beguiled.
The edge of space becomes a stage,
For Zorp to shine, a cosmic mage!

With laughter and light, they frolic and play,
Moments of joy fill the Milky Way.
Waving goodbye as it zooms out of sight,
Zorp leaves a trail of sparkles so bright!

Echoes of Solar Winds

In the void, a rock did bounce,
Singing songs, it made us pounce.
With a wiggle and a spin,
It danced around, let the fun begin!

Space junk joined the silly show,
Whirling fast, in a cosmic flow.
A comet laughed, a star blinked bright,
As they all played tag in the night!

Galaxies laughed at the ruckus made,
Throwing in snacks, a cosmic parade.
With meteor showers showering cheer,
They partied on, year after year!

But what's that? It's a giant clump,
Tripping over, oh what a thump!
Dust clouds giggle, and planets shake,
Let's keep it fun, for laughter's sake!

Twilight of the Cosmic Forge

In the forge where stars are born,
A silly sun gets quite forlorn.
With a wiggle and a frown,
He accidentally turned himself down!

The cosmos giggled, couldn't believe,
As stardust fell from a cosmic sleeve.
Supernovae threw confetti so bright,
And Saturn wore party hats all night!

Alien chefs stirred up some stew,
In a pot made from old space debris too.
Jupiter jumped, Uranus twirled,
As they feasted 'round the endless world!

Through the twilight, laughter rang,
Celestial pals in a cosmic clang.
They toasted their quirks, so bold and true,
In a universe where fun always flew!

Journey of Cosmic Travelers

Two comets with tails so bright,
Set off for a galactic flight.
With space goggles all askew,
They grinned wide, shouting, "Yahoo!"

Through asteroid fields, they spun and twirled,
With laughter echoing through the world.
Dodging rocks with goofy flair,
Chasing stardust through the cosmic air!

In a black hole, they took a chance,
Hoping for a gravity dance.
But instead of swirling down,
They made their way back around town!

So off they went, two jolly pals,
Riding waves of cosmic gales.
And in the end, their tales expanded,
For smiles and fun are just as planned!

Cosmic Legends

Once there were legends in the sky,
With funny tales that made you cry.
A moon with ears, a star with feet,
Danced through the night to a funky beat!

Space whales sang in harmony sweet,
While black holes played a tricky cheat.
Galactic gossip spread like fire,
As the cosmos sparked with endless desire!

Aliens wearing wacky hats,
Swap space pies with smiling bats.
In a twinkling, they'd laugh and cheer,
Creating memories year after year!

So gather 'round for a playful tale,
Of cosmic fun that will prevail.
For in the vastness, through thick and thin,
The joy of space is where we begin!

The Comet's Lament

I zipped through space, so fast and bright,
But forgot my tail, oh what a fright!
They call me fierce but I'm just a clown,
Got sidetracked by a Martian town.

In cosmic dust, I lost my way,
My shine now dimmed, oh what a fray!
Gravity pulls and I lose my grace,
Chasing aliens in a silly race.

With hiccups loud, I crack and pop,
My friends just laugh, they can't stop!
A comet's woe, it's truly a scene,
In this grand ballet, I'm the king of the mean.

So if you see me dart and sway,
Just know I'm lost, and here to play!
With cosmic giggles I'll leave a trace,
The universe dancin' in absolute space.

Whispers of the Interstellar Drift

Floating by in a cosmic breeze,
I heard some gossip from the stars with ease.
They chuckled loud at the sun's big hair,
Even the planets, they found it quite rare.

Uranus told a joke, had us all in tears,
While Venus danced, igniting our fears.
The black hole guffawed, what a sight to see,
As Saturn's rings spun in jubilee.

With each passing moon, secrets take flight,
In galactic corners, where shadows delight.
The whispers of laughter, they twirl in the void,
As stardust giggles, a moment enjoyed.

Oh, the tales of the drift, they never grow old,
With cosmic friendships and stories retold.
So let's drift together, on this merry ride,
In the sea of the stars, let joy be our guide.

Guardians of the Cosmic Abyss

In the void, where the funny things hide,
The Guardians laugh, always side by side.
With capes made of stardust, they twirl and flip,
Protecting the cosmos with a giggly grip.

Zipping past meteors, they throw confetti,
While chasing rogue comets, the fun gets quite heady.
They tickle the asteroids, watch them disperse,
In the vast cosmic pool, there's never a curse.

"Watch out for black holes!" one Guardian cried,
But instead of fear, it's a joy ride!
They loop and they whirl, in a blissful spin,
For guardians of laughter, always win!

So if you're ever lost in the ether's embrace,
Just peek at the Guardians and join in their grace.
Life is a party, in the great cosmic sea,
Laughter's the key, just glide, wild and free.

Dust and Dreams Among the Stars

In a swirl of dust, my dreams take flight,
Bouncing on comets, oh what a sight!
With giggles galore in the stardust brew,
I paint the night sky in colors anew.

Shooting stars whisper, tickling my ear,
"Join us for laughter, banish all fear!"
We waltz through the meteors, grand galactic ball,
Where the punchline erupts, and we all have a ball.

In dreams made of starlight, I find my bliss,
With a cosmic twist, not one star to miss.
The universe chuckles, a splendid delight,
As we dance on the rings in the soft, silvery light.

So gather your dreams, let them spin like a kite,
In the dust of the cosmos, let laughter ignite.
Together we'll sail, far beyond the far,
With whispers of joy, oh the wonders that are!

Eulogy for a Distant Traveler

In a rocket ship made of cheese,
Our buddy zoomed off with such ease.
He waved goodbye from far away,
While we feasted on chips and hay.

He left Earth with snacks galore,
Munching stardust, what a score!
His spaceship squeaked, his laughter roared,
Now we wish he'd just ignored.

He thought he'd meet some Martian friends,
But they asked him for some trends.
Poor guy just wanted to eat pie,
Instead, he had to learn to fly!

So here's a cheer for his strange ride,
In space where no one can abide.
He might be lost and made of dreams,
But we'll remember his silly schemes.

The Starry Path of Wanderlust

With a twinkle and a mighty blast,
Off he went, no need to ask.
His map was drawn in crayon bright,
Chasing comets through the night.

He packed his socks and bubblegum,
Determined to find where fun comes from.
He tripped through rings of Saturn's glow,
While aliens cheered, 'Go, buddy, go!'

His shoes left traces of candy crumbs,
As he danced through cosmic drums.
The stars all giggled, planets spun,
In their celestial game of fun.

In the sky, he made his bed,
With meteorites as pillow spread.
Though he wanders, far and wide,
His heart and laughter still abide.

Chronicles of Celestial Dust

Once there lived a dust mote bold,
Who traveled tales that needed told.
He surfed on beams of sunlit grace,
With giggling stars that set the pace.

He spun in rings, danced with delight,
Fell in love with a moonbeam bright.
But when he tried to take her home,
She said, 'Oh no! I can't, I roam!'

Around black holes, he twirled and spun,
With wishes whispered, oh so fun.
He gathered stories from the breeze,
And tickled planets with his tease.

In the end, he learned a trick,
To make the galaxies laugh and tick.
His legacy, a cosmic jest,
Reminds us all, we're truly blessed.

When Heaven Weeps in Stone

A boulder once fell from the sky,
With a heavy sigh, it said goodbye.
It tumbled down, with a clumsy cheer,
And left a crater, oh so dear!

It tried to bounce but squashed a flower,
And in that moment, felt the power.
It rolled on through the town so proud,
While giggling kids surrounded the crowd.

"Oh look!" they cried, "A rock that speaks!"
"It tells of myths in funny squeaks!"
They poked and prodded, what a scene,
A stone who dreamt of being a queen!

At sunset's glow, it found its fame,
For making laughter, that was its game.
So now it sits, a star so bright,
In our hearts, a boulder of light.

Tides of Galactic Winds

In the cosmos, a bump was found,
A wandering rock with a silly sound.
It rolled and tumbled, full of cheer,
Cheeky space rocks, I must revere.

With every twist and every spin,
It plays a game, it's hard to win.
Slipping through stars, it giggles bright,
A cosmic prankster in the night.

A dance with comets, a lunar waltz,
Bumping into planets, oh, what a fault!
The universe laughs at this clumsy tease,
As gravity pulls with such great ease.

Oh, the tales of rocks so bold and brash,
They zoom and glide, they swish and clash.
In the vastness with endless spins,
Wandering gems in forgotten bins.

The Dance of the Wandering Lights

Twinkling far, like distant laughs,
When lights collide, it writes new paths.
They jig and jive, a ball of glee,
Dancing around in a cosmic spree.

Watch them sway in a wink and blink,
Tip-toeing on the edge of a drink.
Stars masquerade in a shimmering show,
As lights embrace like a cosmic glow.

One sneezes bright, the others duck,
Falling back with such bad luck.
They swirl and twirl, making haste,
A game of bumper stars, what a taste!

In laughter they twinkle, this party entwines,
With echoes and giggles through celestial pines.
The universe grins at their silly play,
A dance of lights, come join, hooray!

Celestial Memoirs

From ages past, the rocks confide,
In tales that loop and silly ride.
They scribble notes with tails aflame,
A history written in cosmic fame.

Each meteor's secret, a jest they share,
Of how they got stuck in cosmic fare.
One thought it a race but tripped on a moon,
And landed with flair to a comical tune.

Planets chuckle at stories untold,
While stars gather round, feeling bold.
With giggles they chime in the dark,
A book of the skies, oh what a lark!

Lost in the echoes of cosmic scribes,
Where laughter abounds, and joy resides.
These memos of space, both wild and wry,
Are read by the suns that dance in the sky.

Chronicles of the Celestial Plains

On the grand expanse of stellar dunes,
Nibbling on cosmic marshmallow moons.
Rocks play frisbee with shooting stars,
While black holes laugh from afar.

The universe quips with tales so bright,
Of aliens pranking under starlit night.
They hide in craters, play peek-a-boo,
While planets engage in an interstellar stew.

"Catch me if you can!" a comet cries,
Zooming past with mischievous eyes.
Galactic races over red dust trails,
In the playground of space, laughter prevails.

So gather around, from worlds afar,
For a saga of snacks on a shooting star.
The plains of the cosmos resonate cheer,
With tales of fun that we hold dear.

Beyond the Celestial Horizon

In the sky where rock stars play,
Bouncing off the Milky Way,
An errant chunk rolled on its way,
Waving at the sun's bouquet.

Space tourists forgetting their rhyme,
Paid in stardust, they float in time,
One asked for snacks, 'Oh, what a crime!'
As comets danced in perfect mime.

With thrills and spins, they left their trace,
Embarrassed, a moon hid its face,
While meteors skated with grace,
They all cheered for space's embrace.

So let's hoot and holler tonight,
For wandering rocks that ignite,
In cosmic parties, oh what a sight,
As stars wink in delight, pure light!

The Pursuit of Celestial Dreams

There was a dreamer from Mars,
Who wanted to dance with the stars,
He tripped on a meteor's flare,
And ended up stuck in space's bazaar.

He tried on a comet's long tail,
But it was too heavy to sail,
He giggled and gave it a twirl,
Saying, 'Who knew space could unfurl?'

When aliens joined in the fun,
They laughed 'til their sides felt undone,
Trading bright rocks for an old shoe,
Even space goes wacky for a few!

So toast to the dreams of the night,
In galactic gatherings so bright,
As we reach for the stars in our lane,
Let's bubble with joy in the cosmic rain!

The Forgotten Comets

Once there were comets, so proud,
Glowing bright, they drew a crowd,
But then they forgot their own names,
And started playing silly games.

One thought it cool to disguise,
With glitter and googly eyes,
But who would believe what they see?
A comet dressed as a bumblebee!

Another spun round in circles tight,
Claiming it was the dance of the night,
With asteroids cheering, oh what fun,
'The stars have all lost track, everyone!'

So here's to the forgotten crew,
Who boogie and sway in the cosmic zoo,
With laughter that echoes through space,
They'll remain the funny ones in this race!

The Lure of the Celestial Highway

On the highway of stars, they zoom,
Chasing light 'round the moon's big room,
With bumper stickers like 'I Love Space',
They'll race through the cosmos, finding their place.

They pit stop at Saturn for milkshakes,
And twirl with the rings like little flakes,
While Jupiter's moons jump in for a spin,
Shouting, 'Come on, let the fun begin!'

With a wink from a nebula up high,
They trade tales of why they'd fly,
One says he needs to groom his tail,
While others just want to live without fail.

So buckle up for a trip, my friend,
In this wacky ride, the giggles never end,
As laughter echoes through the starry maze,
On the cosmic highway, we'll sparkle in praise!

Echoes of the Iron Giants

Metal men in a dance, shaped by cosmic chance,
They wobble and sway, in a space-time romance.
With rusty old screws and creaky old gears,
They giggle and guffaw, defying our fears.

In zero-G jiggles, they bounce off the walls,
One's tripped on a rock, now hilariously sprawls.
They hoot like lost robots, so silly and spry,
Who knew space could bring such a clumsy guy?

Every crash is a hoot, every drift is a tease,
They twirl through the stars, like leaves in the breeze.
With a clang and a clatter, they try to align,
But with every grand plan, it's chaos divine.

So here's to the giants, who dance and who play,
Their cosmic ballet in the milky way.
In a universe vast, they twinkle in laughter,
Their echoes will linger, forever hereafter.

When Stars Collide

In a cosmic crash, what a sight to behold,
Stars meet with a boom, as the legends foretold.
They tumble and tumble, like kids on a swing,
Giggles erupt as they dance like a fling.

With a wink and a wink, they share silly tales,
Of comets gone wild and space-time snails.
In the chaos of sparks, they form a new face,
A giggling galaxy, an interstellar embrace.

"Oh dear," says a nova, "I've spilled all my juice!"
"Let's play tag through the dark!" says the brave supermoose.
With a sparkle and spin, they race through the night,
Creating new worlds, what a cosmic delight!

So when you look up, with wonder and cheer,
Know it's just laughter echoing near.
Stars crashing and clashing, it's all in the game,
A raucous celestial circus—we'll never be the same!

Journey Through the Void

Through the void they zipped, a parade of bright lights,
Galactic funfair, with carnival sights.
With blusters and booms, they laughed 'till they cried,
What a wild ride through the cosmic slide!

They jostled and tussled, with asteroids funny,
Launching from galaxies, dripping with honey.
One slipped on a comet, ricocheted like a seed,
Pooling in stardust, oh yes, what a lead!

"Hold on tight!" they yelled, as they weaved through the space,
Dodging black holes with a giggling grace.
Strange little critters waved flags made of dreams,
While laughter erupted in glittering beams.

Their journey was filled with bizarre, jolly sights,
Shooting stars juggling, and moon-monkeys in tights.
When they reached the end, they all danced aside,
Through the void and beyond, on a whimsical ride!

Fragments of Forgotten Worlds

In the remnants of worlds, where laughter once thrived,
The echoes of jokes and fun still survived.
With pieces of dreams, and giggles galore,
They bounce round like balls, on a cosmic floor.

"Remember that time?" a comet takes flight,
"Chased by a planet, we danced through the night!"
With fragments of laughter, they gathered and spun,
In the silence of space, they continued to run.

Odd little relics, like silly old jesters,
Filled with the quirks of their long-lost conquests.
They twinkle and wink, sharing tales of their plight,
In a galaxy where fun is a flickering light.

So cherish the fragments; they can't break apart,
For laughter in space is a cosmic art.
As long as they chuckle, and reminisce bowled,
These fragments will shimmer, forever retold.

The Celestial Odyssey

A rock in the sky, just passing through,
With a goofy grin, it waves at you.
It tumbles and rolls, oh what a dance,
Making wishes on dreams with a cosmic glance.

It skipped by the moon, gave the sun a poke,
Said, 'I'm a space rock, but I'm no joke!'
Laughing with stars in a silly race,
Chasing the trails of a cheeky face.

It lands on Mars, says, 'Hey, what's new?'
Plans a giant picnic, just me and you.
But the Martians just stare, all looking so sly,
As our cosmic friend shouts, 'Pizza from the sky!'

With each bouncy leap, the fun never ends,
It winks at the comets and calls them friends.
In this cosmic circus, forever it'll soar,
A jester in space, always wanting more.

Chasing the Night Sky

There's a rock with a hat, so wobbly and spry,
Zooming around with a glimmering eye.
It giggles with planets and tap dances too,
'Catch me if you can!' it shouts, 'You snooze, you rue!'

With a flip and a flop, it goes round and round,
Spinning star trails that twirl on the ground.
A cosmic caper beneath the bright moon,
The night sky's playground, oh, what a tune!

Chasing the twinkles, it plays hide and seek,
Behind clouds and comets, boisterous and meek.
The stars all giggle, lighting the path,
For this charming rock's adventurous math.

With each little leap, it cheers us to play,
Beaming with joy, making night into day.
In the sky's grand bazaar, fun never fades,
As our cheeky friend jigs through celestial shades.

Remnants of a Starfall

Fell from the heavens, a ball of dust,
With a 'whoops' and a 'yikes', in laughter we trust.
It landed with style, a jittery touch,
'Is this Earth? I like it! It's cozy and such.'

It sparkled and shined, like glitter on toast,
Singing to friends, its post-fall boast.
'Watch me, watch me!' it giggled with glee,
As it rolled down a hill, trying to flee!

Bouncing through trees, it crashes in mud,
Sticking up leaves, creating a flood.
The residents chuckle, saying, 'What's that?'
'Just remnants of fun, no need for a spat!'

Sharing stories of space in a charming way,
With the lessons in laughter, to cheer up the day.
In a world full of whims, this dust piles high,
And the universe chuckles as time rolls by.

Shadows Among the Planets

In the shadows of giants, a pebble sneaks near,
It whispers to Saturn, 'You've got quite a rear!'
Playing peekaboo with asteroids bold,
Sunny and cheeky, never growing old.

It pokes at the moons, throwing dust in their eyes,
'Let's have a party, beneath all these skies!'
With rings all around, it twirls with delight,
As planets roll in for a dance on the night.

Jupiter frowns, 'What a raucous affair!'
But our pebble just beams, 'Come on, if you dare!'
The Milky Way giggles, lighting the way,
As laughter erupts in a cosmic ballet.

With each little waltz, it shines and it bounces,
Cheering for friendship, where joy always pronounces.
Among cosmic shadows, together they sway,
In the laughter of light, they all find their play.

Whispers of Ancient Celestial Wonders

In the sky, rocks roam with glee,
Making faces at us, oh so free.
They play hide and seek with the Sun,
With a wink and a nudge, oh what fun!

One cheeky chunk bumps into a star,
Saying, "Hey, I think I'm a shooting star!"
The star just chuckles, glowing bright,
"You need some polish, you're quite a sight!"

With tales of collisions and dusty trails,
They gossip in whispers, sharing old tales.
Such a cosmic comedy, day by day,
These rocks have jokes, come hear what they say!

So look to the heavens, let laughter unfold,
For even the cosmos has stories to be told.

Through the Eyes of the Milky Way

The galaxy giggles, dainty and spry,
With twinkling stars that seem to sigh.
"Check out that rock, what's its deal?"
"It thinks it's a comet, oh what a reel!"

They swirl in formation, a dance in the dark,
Bumping and wobbling, each with a spark.
Meteors tease, making a fuss,
While planets are rolling, oh what a bus!

One planet yells, "I need some space!"
Another one pokes, "But you're out of place!"
The cosmos just cackles, alive with the scene,
A party in orbit, what a wild dream!

So gaze at the brightness, let your heart sway,
In this whimsical dance, we find our own way.

Onward to the Celestial Abyss

Far beyond, where laughter takes flight,
Lurks a black hole, devouring the light.
It grins with mischief, swirling the night,
"I'll take your stars, now that feels right!"

Asteroids chime in, "Don't be so grim,
We're just rolling by for a cosmic swim!"
They splash in the void, creating a wave,
"Floating away is the life we crave!"

The black hole snickers, "Come closer, dear friend,
You'll see I'm a blast, I just like to pretend!"
Cosmic chuckles echo through the vast,
In this funny vacuum, no need for the fast.

So onward we go, with laughter so bright,
In the depths of the cosmos, all feels just right!

Journeying Beacons of Light

Flickering rays, flirting with space,
Stars play tag with a quirky grace.
"Catch me if you can!" they giggle and blink,
As comets zoom past, in a glitzy pink!

In this light show, where dreams take flight,
Planetary pals twirl in delight.
"Let's hold hands and dance through the dark!"
Said a moon to its buddy, a shimmering spark.

As meteors zoom, they shed a small tear,
"Wishing on you, we hold you so dear!"
With laughter and joy, they embrace the sky,
In their interstellar caper, oh me, oh my!

So here's to the glow, the giggles, and cheer,
Our journey in light spreads laughter so near!

Celestial Wanderers

In space they roam, with flair and style,
Bumping into planets, wearing a smile.
Some take a detour, just for a snack,
Others flip backwards, they've lost their track.

They crash and they laugh, who cares for the laws?
Dodging the stars and cosmic applause.
A game of tag in the void so grand,
Giddy in orbit, no plans pre-planned.

Round and round, like a child on a swing,
Chasing their tails, what joy do they bring!
Gravity's tricky, they float and they spin,
"Catch me if you can!" with a cheeky grin.

They light up the night, mischievous and bold,
With tales of mischief that never get old.
Whirling through the cosmos, wild and free,
Who knew the skies held such lunacy?

Collision of Timelessness

Two wanderers met, out in the black,
With a pop and a sizzle, they staged their attack.
Their cosmic embrace, a clumsy embrace,
They giggled and spun, lost in their chase.

"Oops!" said one, as they tumbled through space,
"This time travel gig is a true rat race!"
Sparks flew like fireworks, bright cosmic fun,
With a wink and a grin, they were on the run.

The clocks were all wrong, but who even cares?
They danced through dimensions—oh, how it flares!
Wobbling through eons, what tales would they spin?
Timelessly tangled, let the party begin!

With giggles and snorts, their chaos amassed,
Stardust giggles, the shadows they cast.
In the cosmic void, where silliness reigns,
Who knew timelessness would come with such gains?

Ride of the Fallen Giants

Once giants of rock, now rolling away,
They laugh as they tumble in cosmic ballet.
"Look at me!" cried one, with a twinkle and spin,
"I'm a star in my own right, come join in my din!"

To hitch a ride on their rocky pride,
You'd need a good sense of humor inside.
From Saturn's rings to the Moon's pleasant glide,
They share silly stories while tossing aside.

With bumps and with thuds, they embrace the thrill,
Who needs to be graceful when you can just chill?
They race with the comets, they tumble and fall,
Silly old giants, just having a ball!

Through cosmic giggles, their laughter is bright,
Fallen skillfully, while dancing with light.
In their journey of fun, boundless and vast,
Of cosmic mischief, they're ever steadfast!

Specters of the Infinite

In shadows they drift, with a mischievous glow,
Whispering secrets from long, long ago.
"Boo!" they all chuckle, in spaces unseen,
The ghosts of the cosmos, so silly, so keen.

Flipping through time like an old faded reel,
They tickle the stars with an ethereal feel.
Haunting the voids where no one dare tread,
They heal with their laughter, so wild and widespread.

They play peek-a-boo with the planets below,
Twinkling like mischief in beautiful flow.
"Join our parade!" they plea with a scare,
What fun is the void if you can't giggle and glare?

Through cosmic capers, they dance with delight,
Specters of humor, lighting the night.
In the infinite wilderness, joy takes its stand,
Together forever—happy, hand-in-hand.

www.ingramcontent.com/pod-product-compliance
Lightning Source LLC
Chambersburg PA
CBHW071822160426
43209CB00003B/178